Monday Night Meals

Delicious Monday Recipes to Start Your Week

By
BookSumo Press
Copyright © by Saxonberg Associates
All rights reserved

Published by
BookSumo Press, a DBA of Saxonberg Associates
http://www.booksumo.com/

ABOUT THE AUTHOR.

BookSumo Press is a publisher of unique, easy, and healthy cookbooks.

Our cookbooks span all topics and all subjects. If you want a deep dive into the possibilities of cooking with any type of ingredient. Then BookSumo Press is your go to place for robust yet simple and delicious cookbooks and recipes. Whether you are looking for great tasting pressure cooker recipes or authentic ethic and cultural food. BookSumo Press has a delicious and easy cookbook for you.

With simple ingredients, and even simpler step-by-step instructions BookSumo cookbooks get everyone in the kitchen chefing delicious meals.

BookSumo is an independent publisher of books operating in the beautiful Garden State (NJ) and our team of chefs and kitchen experts are here to teach, eat, and be merry!

INTRODUCTION

Welcome to *The Effortless Chef Series*! Thank you for taking the time to purchase this cookbook.

Come take a journey into the delights of easy cooking. The point of this cookbook and all BookSumo Press cookbooks is to exemplify the effortless nature of cooking simply.

In this book we focus on cooking on Monday Night. You will find that even though the recipes are simple, the taste of the dishes are quite amazing.

So will you take an adventure in simple cooking? If the answer is yes please consult the table of contents to find the dishes you are most interested in.

Once you are ready, jump right in and start cooking.

— BookSumo Press

Table of Contents

About the Author 2

Introduction 3

Table of Contents 4

Any Issues? Contact Us 8

Legal Notes 9

Common Abbreviations 10

Chapter 1: Easy Monday Night Recipes 11

    Thai Style Noodles 11

    Hearty Chili Noodles Bake 14

    Noodles & Shrimp Asian Style 17

    Noodles Russian Style 20

    Noodles Hungarian Style 22

    Unique Nacho Joes 24

    Super-Bowl Nachos 26

Southwest Nachos 29

Indian Style Fried Chicken 32

Chicken Steaks with Gravy 34

Crispy Chicken Croquettes 37

Fried Chicken & Rice 40

Honey Buttermilk Fried Chicken 43

Barbecued Chipotle Meatloaf 46

Chipotle Mac and Cheese 49

Creamy Chipotle Chicken Sandwich 52

Cheesy Chipotle Lamb Burgers in Maple Glaze 55

Louisiana Paella 58

Hannah's Jambalaya 60

Crossroads Beef 63

Authentic Texas Burgers 65

Spicy Garlic Tilapia 67

Lime and Mushrooms Tilapia 69

Creamy Lemon Pepper Tilapia 71

Monterey Shrimp 73
Szechwan Shrimp 75
Shrimp Scampi 77
Maui Chicken 79
Coconut Chicken 81
Asian Style Chicken with Plums 83
Classical Alfredo 85
Easy Italian Parmigiana 88
Maggie's Favorite Pasta 90
CLASSICAL LASAGNA I 93
CHICKEN MARSALA CLASSICO 96
Chipotle Chili 98
Easy Rustic Chili 101
Turkey, Salsa, and Zucchini Chili 103
Italian Cabbage I 106
Classical Enchiladas 108
Cantonese Ground Beef 110

Lemongrass Beef	113
Italian Cabbage II	115
Sweet and Sour Ground Beef	117
Ground Beef Macaroni	119
Buffalo Wings I	121
Buffalo Chicken Sandwich	124
Buffalo Pizza	126
Florida Style Pierogi	128
Emily's Marsala	130
Panhandle Seafood Sampler	133
Authentic Cuban Sandwich II	136
Classical Spanish Beef Patties	139
THANKS FOR READING! JOIN THE CLUB AND KEEP ON COOKING WITH 6 MORE COOKBOOKS	141
Come On	143
Let's Be Friends :)	143

Any Issues? Contact Us

If you find that something important to you is missing from this book please contact us at info@booksumo.com.

We will take your concerns into consideration when the 2nd edition of this book is published. And we will keep you updated!

— BookSumo Press

LEGAL NOTES

ALL RIGHTS RESERVED. NO PART OF THIS BOOK MAY BE REPRODUCED OR TRANSMITTED IN ANY FORM OR BY ANY MEANS. PHOTOCOPYING, POSTING ONLINE, AND / OR DIGITAL COPYING IS STRICTLY PROHIBITED UNLESS WRITTEN PERMISSION IS GRANTED BY THE BOOK'S PUBLISHING COMPANY. LIMITED USE OF THE BOOK'S TEXT IS PERMITTED FOR USE IN REVIEWS WRITTEN FOR THE PUBLIC.

COMMON ABBREVIATIONS

cup(s)	C.
tablespoon	tbsp
teaspoon	tsp
ounce	oz.
pound	lb

*All units used are standard American measurements

Chapter 1: Easy Monday Night Recipes

Thai Style Noodles

Ingredients

- 4 eggs
- 1 tbsp soy sauce
- 1 tbsp sesame oil
- canola oil
- 1 (12 oz.) package extra-firm tofu, cubed
- 2 C. sliced fresh mushrooms
- 2 C. broccoli florets
- 1/4 C. chopped cashews
- 1 (10 oz.) package frozen shelled edamame (green soybeans)
- 1 (16 oz.) package egg noodles
- 1/2 C. unsweetened soy milk
- 1/2 C. peanut butter
- 1/4 C. reduced-fat coconut milk
- 1 tsp tahini

Directions

- Set your oven to 350 degrees F before doing anything else.
- In a bowl, mix together the soy sauce and eggs.
- Heat a nonstick skillet on medium heat and cook the egg mixture for about 3-5 minutes.

- Transfer the cooked eggs onto a cutting board and chop them.
- In a large skillet, heat both the oils on medium heat and cook the tofu for about 8-10 minutes.
- Transfer the tofu into a bowl.
- In the same skillet, add the broccoli and mushrooms and cook for about 5-7 minutes.
- In a baking dish, place the cashews and cook them in the oven for about 8-12 minutes.
- In a microwave safe bowl, place the edamame and microwave it, covered for about 1-2 minutes.
- In a large pan of lightly salted boiling water, cook the egg noodles for about 8 minutes.
- Drain them well and keep everything aside.
- In a large pan, mix together the remaining ingredients on medium heat and cook, stirring continuously, for about 2-4 minutes.
- Add the noodles, tofu, chopped eggs, edamame and broccoli mixture and toss to combine.
- Serve with a topping of roasted cashews.

Amount per serving (6 total)

Timing Information:

Preparation	30 m
Cooking	35 m
Total Time	1 h 5 m

Nutritional Information:

Calories	695 kcal
Fat	32.9 g
Carbohydrates	70.5g
Protein	35.3 g
Cholesterol	187 mg
Sodium	383 mg

* Percent Daily Values are based on a 2,000 calorie diet.

Hearty Chili Noodles Bake

Ingredients

- 1 (12 oz.) package wide egg noodles
- 1 lb. ground beef
- 1 onion, chopped
- 3 cloves garlic, minced
- 2 (15 oz.) cans tomato sauce
- 1 (8 oz.) can tomato sauce
- 15 fluid oz. water
- 1 C. red wine
- 1 tbsp ground cumin
- 1 tsp dried oregano
- 1/2 tsp cayenne pepper
- 1 C. shredded sharp Cheddar cheese

Directions

- Set your oven to 350 degrees F before doing anything else and grease a 14x9-inch baking dish.
- In a large pan of lightly salted boiling water, cook the egg noodles for about 5 minutes, stirring occasionally.
- Drain them well and keep everything aside.
- Heat a large skillet on medium-high heat and cook the beef till browned completely.
- Add the onion and garlic and stir fry them till the onion becomes tender.

- Add the tomato sauce, wine, water, oregano, cumin and cayenne pepper and bring to a simmer.
- Stir in the pasta and place the mixture into the prepared baking dish.
- Top everything with the cheddar cheese and cook everything in the oven for about 20 minutes.

Amount per serving (6 total)

Timing Information:

Preparation	15 m
Cooking	35 m
Total Time	50 m

Nutritional Information:

Calories	510 kcal
Fat	20 g
Carbohydrates	49g
Protein	27.6 g
Cholesterol	111 mg
Sodium	1129 mg

* Percent Daily Values are based on a 2,000 calorie diet.

Noodles & Shrimp Asian Style

Ingredients

- 1 lb. fresh Chinese egg noodles
- 2 tbsp olive oil
- 1/3 C. chopped onion
- 1 clove garlic, chopped
- 3/4 C. broccoli florets
- 1/2 C. chopped red bell pepper
- 2 C. cooked shrimp
- 1/2 C. sliced water chestnuts, drained
- 1/2 C. baby corn, drained
- 1/2 C. canned sliced bamboo shoots, drained
- 3 tbsp oyster sauce
- 1 tbsp red pepper flakes, or to taste

Directions

- In a large pan of lightly salted boiling water, cook the egg noodles for about 1-2 minutes.
- Drain them well and keep everything aside.
- In a large skillet, heat the oil on medium-high heat, sauté the onion and garlic for about 1 minute.
- Stir in the bell pepper and broccoli and stir fry everything for about 3 minutes.

- Stir in the remaining ingredients and cook for about 3 more minutes.
- Serve the noodles with a topping of the veggie mixture.

Amount per serving (6 total)

Timing Information:

Preparation	20 m
Cooking	10 m
Total Time	30 m

Nutritional Information:

Calories	322 kcal
Fat	6.3 g
Carbohydrates	49g
Protein	15.1 g
Cholesterol	83 mg
Sodium	616 mg

* Percent Daily Values are based on a 2,000 calorie diet.

NOODLES RUSSIAN STYLE

Ingredients

- 1 (8 oz.) package egg noodles
- 2 C. sour cream
- 1/2 C. grated Parmesan cheese, divided
- 1 tbsp chopped fresh chives
- 1/2 tsp salt
- 1/8 tsp ground black pepper
- 2 tbsp butter

Directions

- In a large pan of lightly salted boiling water, cook the egg noodles for about 8-10 minutes.
- Drain well.
- Add the butter and stir to combine.
- Meanwhile in a bowl, mix together 1/4 C. of the cheese, sour cream, chives, salt and black pepper.
- Place the mixture over the noodles and gently, stir to combine.
- Serve immediately with a topping of the remaining cheese.

Amount per serving (6 total)

Timing Information:

Preparation	10 m
Cooking	10 m
Total Time	20 m

Nutritional Information:

Calories	363 kcal
Fat	24.2 g
Carbohydrates	27.1g
Protein	9.9 g
Cholesterol	78 mg
Sodium	394 mg

* Percent Daily Values are based on a 2,000 calorie diet.

NOODLES HUNGARIAN STYLE

Ingredients

- 1 (8 oz.) package fine egg noodles
- 2 C. cottage cheese
- 2 C. sour cream
- 1/2 C. chopped onions
- 2 tbsp Worcestershire sauce
- 2 tbsp poppy seeds
- 1 tsp salt
- 1 tbsp grated Parmesan cheese
- 1 pinch ground paprika

Directions

- Set your oven to 350 degrees F before doing anything else and grease a large casserole dish.
- In a large pan of lightly salted boiling water, cook the egg noodles for about 5 minutes, stirring occasionally.
- Drain them well and keep everything aside.
- In a large bowl, add the noodles and remaining ingredients except the Parmesan cheese and paprika and mix well.
- Transfer the mixture into the prepared casserole dish evenly and top with the Parmesan cheese and paprika.
- Cook everything in the oven for about 30 minutes.

Amount per serving (6 total)

Timing Information:

Preparation	15 m
Cooking	35 m
Total Time	50 m

Nutritional Information:

Calories	414 kcal
Fat	22.6 g
Carbohydrates	35.1g
Protein	18.1 g
Cholesterol	77 mg
Sodium	809 mg

* Percent Daily Values are based on a 2,000 calorie diet.

Unique Nacho Joes

Ingredients

- 1 lb. ground beef
- 1 red onion, diced
- 1 green pepper, diced
- salt, to taste
- pepper, to taste
- 2 tbsp oil
- 2 tbsp garlic, minced
- 2 tsp Worcestershire sauce
- 1 (1 1/4 oz.) envelope taco seasoning
- 1 (16 oz.) jar salsa con queso, medium
- hamburger bun
- tortilla chips, for serving
- sour cream, if desired
- jalapeno pepper, if desired
- salsa, if desired
- shredded cheddar cheese, if desired

Directions

- In a large skillet, heat the oil and sauté the pepper and onion till tender.
- Add the beef, salt and black pepper and cook until it is browned completely. Stir in the garlic, taco seasoning and Worcestershire sauce and bring to a gentle simmer. Reduce the heat to low and stir in the salsa. Simmer for about 15 minutes. Place the beef mixture over the buns alongside the jalapenos, sour cream and cheese or salsa.

Amount per serving: 4

Timing Information:

| Preparation | 10 mins |
| Total Time | 30 mins |

Nutritional Information:

Calories	329.5
Fat	23.9g
Cholesterol	77.1mg
Sodium	105.0mg
Carbohydrates	6.0g
Protein	21.8g

* Percent Daily Values are based on a 2,000 calorie diet.

SUPER-BOWL NACHOS

Ingredients

- 2 large russet potatoes, scrubbed and chopped into thick wedges
- 2 -3 tsp vegetable oil
- 1/4 tsp garlic powder
- 1 tsp taco seasoning
- 1/4 C. black beans, rinsed and drained
- 2 tsp lime juice
- 1/4 tsp cumin
- 1/4 tsp chili powder
- cayenne pepper, to taste
- 1/2 medium tomatoes, diced
- 1 green onion, chopped
- 1 tbsp green chili, diced
- 2 tbsp shredded 4-cheese Mexican blend cheese

Directions

- Set your oven to 425 degrees F before doing anything else.
- In a baking dish, add the potatoes, taco seasoning, garlic powder and oil and toss to coat well.
- Now, place the potato wedges in a single layer and cook everything in the oven for about 25-30 minutes, stirring occasionally.
- Meanwhile in a pan, mix together the black beans, lime juice and spices on medium-low heat.
- Cook, stirring occasionally till majority of the liquid is absorbed.

- Remove everything from the heat and stir in the tomato, green chili and green onion.
- Remove the potatoes from the oven and immediately, sprinkle them with the cheese.
- Cook everything in the oven for about 1-2 minutes more.
- Top the potato wedges with the bean mixture and serve.

Amount per serving: 2

Timing Information:

Preparation	20 mins
Total Time	55 mins

Nutritional Information:

Calories	397.5
Fat	7.5g
Cholesterol	8.4mg
Sodium	158.8mg
Carbohydrates	73.3g
Protein	11.7g

* Percent Daily Values are based on a 2,000 calorie diet.

Southwest Nachos

Ingredients

- 1 C. diced tomatoes
- 1/4 C. diced green pepper
- 2 tbsp chopped ripe olives
- 2 tbsp chopped green chilies
- 2 tsp white vinegar
- 1/4 tsp garlic powder
- 1/8 tsp fresh ground pepper
- corn tortilla chips
- 1/4 C. shredded low-fat sharp cheddar cheese
- Corn Tortilla Chips
- 9 6-inch corn tortillas
- cold water

Directions

- Set your oven to 350 degrees F before doing anything else.
- Dip the tortillas in the cold water and then drain them on paper towels.
- Arrange the tortillas onto an ungreased baking sheet and cook everything in the oven for about 10 minutes.
- Remove everything from the oven and keep it aside to cool.
- With a biscuit cutter, cut the tortillas into 2 1/2-inch circles.
- Now, set the oven to broiler and arrange the oven rack about 6-inches from the heating element.

- In a large bowl, mix together the olives, green pepper, tomatoes, green chilies, garlic powder, black pepper and vinegar.
- Place about 2 tsp of the vegetables mixture on each tortilla chips and cook everything under the broiler till the cheese is melted.

Amount per serving: 1

Timing Information:

| Preparation | 10 mins |
| Total Time | 20 mins |

Nutritional Information:

Calories	18.9
Fat	0.3g
Cholesterol	0.2mg
Sodium	14.8mg
Carbohydrates	3.4g
Protein	0.7g

* Percent Daily Values are based on a 2,000 calorie diet.

Indian Style Fried Chicken

Ingredients

- 1 (4 lb.) whole chicken, cut into pieces
- 6 cloves garlic, chopped
- 4 tbsp oyster sauce
- 2 tbsp curry powder
- 1/2 C. vegetable oil

Directions

- In a glass dish, mix together the oyster sauce, garlic and curry powder.
- Add the chicken pieces and coat it with the mixture generously.
- Cover and refrigerate for at least 1/2 hour.
- In a large skillet, heat the oil on medium-high heat and fry the chicken pieces for about 20-25 minutes

Amount per serving (4 total)

Timing Information:

Preparation	15 m
Cooking	25 m
Total Time	1 h 15 m

Nutritional Information:

Calories	1238 kcal
Fat	96.3 g
Carbohydrates	13.8g
Protein	85.2 g
Cholesterol	1340 mg
Sodium	1430 mg

* Percent Daily Values are based on a 2,000 calorie diet.

Chicken Steaks with Gravy

Ingredients

- 4 (1/2 lb.) chicken cube steaks
- 2 C. all-purpose flour
- 2 tsp baking powder
- 1 tsp baking soda
- 1 tsp black pepper
- 3/4 tsp salt
- 1 1/2 C. buttermilk
- 1 egg
- 1 tbsp hot pepper sauce
- 2 cloves garlic, minced
- 3 C. vegetable shortening for deep frying
- 1/4 C. all-purpose flour
- 4 C. milk
- kosher salt and ground black pepper to taste

Directions

- With a meat pounder, pound the steaks to 1/4-inch thickness.
- In a shallow dish, mix together the flour, baking soda, baking powder, salt and black pepper.
- In another shallow dish, add the egg, buttermilk, hot sauce and garlic and beat well.
- Coat the steaks with the flour mixture then dip in the egg mixture and again coat with the flour mixture.

- In a large skillet, heat the oil to 325 degrees F.
- Add the steaks and fry for about 3-5 minutes on both sides.
- Transfer the steaks onto paper towel lined plates to drain.
- Drain the fat from the skillet, reserving about 1/4 C. of the mixture in the skillet.
- Slowly, add the remaining flour, stirring continuously in the skillet on medium-low heat.
- Slowly, add the milk, stirring continuously and increase the heat to medium.
- Bring to a gentle simmer and cook for about 6-7 minutes.
- Stir in the salt and black pepper and remove from the heat.
- Pour the gravy over the chicken and serve.

Amount per serving (4 total)

Timing Information:

Preparation	20 m
Cooking	20 m
Total Time	40 m

Nutritional Information:

Calories	791 kcal
Fat	34.3 g
Carbohydrates	71.1g
Protein	47 g
Cholesterol	124 mg
Sodium	1393 mg

* Percent Daily Values are based on a 2,000 calorie diet.

Crispy Chicken Croquettes

Ingredients

- 1/4 C. butter
- 1/4 C. flour
- 1/2 C. milk
- 1/2 C. chicken broth
- 3 C. finely chopped cooked chicken
- 1 1/2 C. seasoned bread crumbs, divided
- 2 eggs, beaten
- 1/4 C. minced onion
- 1 tbsp dried parsley
- 1/4 tsp garlic powder
- 1/8 tsp celery seed
- 1/8 tsp cayenne pepper
- salt and ground black pepper to taste
- 1/4 C. oil, or as needed

Directions

- In a pan, melt the butter on medium heat.
- Slowly, add the flour, stirring continuously and cook for about 1 minute.
- Slowly, add the broth and the milk, beating continuously.
- Cook, stirring continuously for about 5-10 minute till a thick sauce forms.
- Remove everything from the heat and keep aside for about 10 minutes to cool.

- In a large bowl, add the cooled sauce, chicken, eggs, 1 C. of the breadcrumbs, onion, parsley, celery seeds, garlic powder, salt and black pepper and mix till well combined.
- Cover and refrigerate to marinate for about 2 hours.
- Make 6 equal sized patties from the mixture.
- In a shallow, dish place the remaining breadcrumbs.
- Roll the each patty in the breadcrumbs.
- In a large skillet, heat the oil on medium-high heat and cook the patties for about 5 minutes per side.
- Transfer the chicken onto paper towel lined plates to drain.

Amount per serving (6 total)

Timing Information:

Preparation	25 m
Cooking	30 m
Total Time	2 h 55 m

Nutritional Information:

Calories	377 kcal
Fat	17.5 g
Carbohydrates	26.6g
Protein	27 g
Cholesterol	137 mg
Sodium	765 mg

* Percent Daily Values are based on a 2,000 calorie diet.

Fried Chicken & Rice

Ingredients

- 3 tbsp oyster sauce
- 2 tbsp fish sauce
- 1 tsp white sugar
- 1/2 C. peanut oil for frying
- 4 C. cooked jasmine rice, chilled
- 6 large cloves garlic clove, crushed
- 2 serrano peppers, crushed
- 1 lb. boneless, skinless chicken breast, cut into thin strips
- 1 red pepper, seeded and thinly sliced
- 1 onion, thinly sliced
- 2 C. sweet Thai basil
- 1 cucumber, sliced
- 1/2 C. cilantro sprigs

Directions

- In a bowl, add the fish sauce, oyster sauce and sugar and beat till well combined.
- In a large skillet, heat the oil on medium-high heat and sauté the serrano pepper and garlic for a while.
- Stir in the chicken strips, sugar mixture, onion and bell pepper and stir fry till the chicken becomes golden brown.

- Increase the heat to high and add in the rice and stir fry till the rice is blended with the chicken mixture.
- Stir in the basil and immediately remove everything from the heat.
- Serve with a garnishing of cucumber and cilantro.

Amount per serving (6 total)

Timing Information:

Preparation	30 m
Cooking	10 m
Total Time	40 m

Nutritional Information:

Calories	794 kcal
Fat	22.1 g
Carbohydrates	116.4g
Protein	29.1 g
Cholesterol	46 mg
Sodium	469 mg

* Percent Daily Values are based on a 2,000 calorie diet.

Honey Buttermilk Fried Chicken

Ingredients

- 3 C. cold water
- 1/4 C. kosher salt
- 1/4 C. honey
- 4 boneless skinless chicken breast halves
- 1/4 C. buttermilk
- 1 C. all-purpose flour
- 1 tsp black pepper
- 1/2 tsp garlic salt
- 1/2 tsp onion salt
- cayenne pepper to taste
- vegetable oil for frying

Directions

- In a large bowl, add the water, honey and salt and mix till the honey is dissolved.
- Add the chicken breast halves and coat with the honey mixture generously and place a heavy plate over the chicken to submerge it completely.
- Cover and refrigerate everything to marinate for about 1 hour.
- Remove the chicken breast halves from the marinade and pat it dry with a paper towel and transfer the meat to a bowl.
- Add the buttermilk and keep it aside for about 15 minutes.

- In a shallow dish, place the flour, onion salt, garlic salt, cayenne pepper, salt and black pepper.
- Coat the chicken breast halves with the flour mixture evenly and arrange everything on a wire rack for about 15 minutes.
- In a large skillet, heat the oil to 350 degrees F and fry the chicken breast halves for about 15-20 minutes.
- Transfer the chicken onto paper towel lined plates to drain.

Amount per serving (4 total)

Timing Information:

Preparation	10 m
Cooking	15 m
Total Time	1 h 45 m

Nutritional Information:

Calories	481 kcal
Fat	21.5 g
Carbohydrates	49.4g
Protein	22.8 g
Cholesterol	65 mg
Sodium	6378 mg

* Percent Daily Values are based on a 2,000 calorie diet.

BARBECUED CHIPOTLE MEATLOAF

Ingredients

- 2 eggs
- 1/3 C. hickory flavored barbeque sauce
- 2 cloves garlic, minced, or to taste
- 2 chipotle chilies in adobo sauce, minced, or to taste
- 2 tbsps adobo sauce from chipotle peppers
- 1 tsp kosher salt
- 1 tsp coarse ground black pepper
- 1/2 tsp celery salt
- 1/2 tsp ground cumin
- 1 tbsp Worcestershire sauce
- 1 onion, chopped
- 1/2 C. dry oatmeal
- 2 pounds lean ground beef
- 2 tbsps hickory flavored barbeque sauce

Directions

- Set your oven to 350 degrees F before doing anything else and grease a 9x5-inch loaf pan.
- In a large bowl, crack the eggs and beat till smooth.
- Add 1/3 C. of barbecue sauce, adobo sauce, Worcestershire sauce, chipotle chilis, garlic, cumin, celery salt, kosher salt and black pepper and beat till well combined.

- Add beef, oatmeal and onion and mix till well combined and transfer into the prepared loaf pan evenly and coat the top with the remaining barbecue sauce.
- Cook in the oven for about 1 hour or till done completely.

Amount per serving (8 total)

Timing Information:

Preparation	15 m
Cooking	1 h
Total Time	1 h 15 m

Nutritional Information:

Calories	306 kcal
Fat	16.2 g
Carbohydrates	12.7g
Protein	25.8 g
Cholesterol	124 mg
Sodium	635 mg

* Percent Daily Values are based on a 2,000 calorie diet.

Chipotle Mac and Cheese

Ingredients

- 1 pound elbow macaroni, cooked according to package directions

Sauce:

- 1 quart half and half, divided
- 1 chipotle pepper from canned chipotles in adobo sauce, or more to taste
- 5 chicken bouillon cubes
- 3 cloves fresh garlic, roughly chopped
- 1 tbsp Spice Islands(R) Onion Powder
- 1/2 tsp Spice Islands(R) Fine Grind Black Pepper (optional)
- 1/4 C. Argo(R) OR Kingsford's(R) Corn Starch
- 2 C. shredded Monterey Jack cheese
- 2 C. shredded pepperjack cheese
- Topping:
- 1 C. shredded pepper jack cheese OR sprinkle with Spice Islands(R) Paprika

Directions

- Set your oven to 350 degrees F before doing anything else and grease a 13x9-inch casserole dish.

- In a food processor or blender, add half-and-half, chipotle peppers, garlic and bouillon and pulse till well combined.
- Transfer the mixture into a large pan with the remaining half-and-half, cornstarch, onion powder and black pepper.
- Bring to a boil, stirring continuously and boil for about 1 minute or till thick and immediately remove from heat.
- Immediately, add cheese and stir till melted completely and then stir in the cooked macaroni.
- Transfer the mixture into the prepared casserole dish evenly and top with the desired topping evenly.
- Cook everything in the oven for about 25-30 minutes or till the top becomes bubbly and golden brown.

Amount per serving (10 total)

Timing Information:

Preparation	20 m
Cooking	30 m
Total Time	50 m

Nutritional Information:

Calories	556 kcal
Fat	31.5 g
Carbohydrates	44.2g
Protein	23.3 g
Cholesterol	98 mg
Sodium	986 mg

* Percent Daily Values are based on a 2,000 calorie diet.

Creamy Chipotle Chicken Sandwich

Ingredients

- 2 tsps olive oil
- 4 skinless, boneless chicken breast halves
- 1 tbsp red wine vinegar
- 1 tbsp fresh lime juice
- 1/2 tsp white sugar
- salt and ground black pepper to taste
- 1 green onion, chopped
- 1 clove garlic, minced
- 1/2 tsp dried oregano
- 1/3 C. light mayonnaise
- 1 tbsp canned chipotle peppers in adobo sauce, seeded and minced
- 1 1/2 tbsps chopped green onion
- 1 1/2 tbsps sweet pickle relish
- 8 slices sourdough bread
- 4 slices mozzarella cheese
- 1 C. torn lettuce

Directions

- In a large skillet, heat the oil on medium heat and sear the chicken breasts for about 10 minutes per side or till browned.
- Stir in 1 tsp lime juice, vinegar, garlic, green onion, sugar, oregano, salt and black pepper and cook for about 5 minutes per side.

- Transfer the chicken mixture into a plate and cover with a piece of foil to keep warm.
- In a blender, add chipotle pepper and mayonnaise and pulse till smooth.
- In a bowl, mix together chipotle mayonnaise, sweet pickle relish and remaining green onion.
- Toast the slices of bread.
- Spread chipotle mayonnaise over 4 bread slices evenly.
- Divide lettuce over the remaining 4 bread slices evenly, followed by 1 chicken breast and 1 cheese slice.
- Cover with the slices of mayonnaise to make a sandwich and serve immediately.

Amount per serving (4 total)

Timing Information:

Preparation	15 m
Cooking	30 m
Total Time	45 m

Nutritional Information:

Calories	451 kcal
Fat	17.3 g
Carbohydrates	35.2g
Protein	37.7 g
Cholesterol	92 mg
Sodium	757 mg

* Percent Daily Values are based on a 2,000 calorie diet.

Cheesy Chipotle Lamb Burgers in Maple Glaze

Ingredients

- 1 head garlic
- 1 pound ground lamb
- 6 oz. soft goat cheese
- 6 tbsps minced chipotle peppers in adobo sauce
- 2 sprigs chopped fresh rosemary
- 2 tbsps maple syrup
- 1 1/2 tsps salt
- 1/2 tsp cracked black pepper
- 1 tbsp olive oil
- 2 tbsps maple syrup
- 4 ciabatta buns, split and toasted

Directions

- Set your oven to 300 degrees F before doing anything else.
- Cut the top of the garlic head and arrange it in a small baking dish and cook it in the oven for about 1 hour or till golden brown.
- Remove everything from the oven and let it cool completely.
- In a bowl, squeeze the garlic head completely.

- Add the lamb, 2 tbsps of maple syrup, goat cheese, chipotle peppers, rosemary, salt and black pepper and mix till well combined and make 4 equal sized patties from the mixture.
- In a large skillet, heat the oil on medium-high heat and cook the patties for about 1 minute per side.
- Reduce the heat to medium-low and cook the patties for about 2 minutes per side or till the desired doneness.
- Just before the last minute of cooking, add the remaining maple syrup.
- Serve these patties in the buns.

Amount per serving (4 total)

Timing Information:

Preparation	40 m
Cooking	1 h 5 m
Total Time	2 h 15 m

Nutritional Information:

Calories	609 kcal
Fat	33.7 g
Carbohydrates	42g
Protein	33.5 g
Cholesterol	110 mg
Sodium	1482 mg

* Percent Daily Values are based on a 2,000 calorie diet.

Louisiana Paella

Ingredients

- 2 tbsps olive oil
- 4 chicken leg quarters
- 2 (8 oz.) packages dirty rice mix
- 5 C. water
- 2 lbs whole cooked crawfish, peeled
- 3/4 medium shrimp, peeled and deveined
- 1/2 lb andouille sausage, sliced into rounds
- 2 C. sliced mushrooms
- 1 large green bell pepper, chopped
- 1 large sweet onion, chopped
- 3 cloves garlic, diced

Directions

- Get your oil hot in a big pot then add in the chicken and brown the meat all over.
- Now add the water and the rice.
- Stir the mix then add in the garlic, crawfish, onion, shrimp, bell peppers, mushrooms, and sausage.
- Get everything boiling while stirring.
- Once the mix is boiling, place a lid on the pot, set the heat to low, and let the paella cook for 35 mins. Enjoy.

Amount per serving (6 total)

Timing Information:

Preparation	30 m
Cooking	45 m
Total Time	1 h 15 m

Nutritional Information:

Calories	757 kcal
Fat	30.5 g
Carbohydrates	62.8g
Protein	54.6 g
Cholesterol	1277 mg
Sodium	1867 mg

* Percent Daily Values are based on a 2,000 calorie diet.

Hannah's Jambalaya

Ingredients

- 2 tbsps peanut oil, divided
- 1 tbsp Cajun seasoning
- 10 oz. andouille sausage, sliced into rounds
- 1 lb boneless skinless chicken breasts, cut into 1 inch pieces
- 1 onion, diced
- 1 small green bell pepper, diced
- 2 stalks celery, diced
- 3 cloves garlic, diced
- 1 (16 oz.) can crushed Italian tomatoes
- 1/2 tsp red pepper flakes
- 1/2 tsp ground black pepper
- 1 tsp salt
- 1/2 tsp hot pepper sauce
- 2 tsps Worcestershire sauce
- 1 tsp file powder
- 1 1/4 C. uncooked white rice
- 2 1/2 C. chicken broth

Directions

- Coat your chicken and sausage with the Cajun spice and fry the sausage in 1 tbsp of peanut oil until everything is browned then remove it from the pan.
- Pour in another tbsp of peanut oil and begin to brown your chicken on all sides. Then place the chicken to the side as well.

- Begin to stir fry your garlic, onions, celery, and bell peppers until the onions are soft then add in the file powder, red pepper, Worcestershire, black pepper, hot sauce, and salt.
- Stir the spices then add in the crushed tomatoes.
- Stir the mix again then add in the sausage and chicken.
- Let the mix cook for 13 mins then add the broth and the rice as well.
- Get the mix boiling, set the heat to low, and let the contents cook for 22 mins.
- Enjoy.

Amount per serving (6 total)

Timing Information:

Preparation	20 m
Cooking	45 m
Total Time	1 h 5 m

Nutritional Information:

Calories	465 kcal
Fat	19.8 g
Carbohydrates	42.4g
Protein	28.1 g
Cholesterol	73 mg
Sodium	1633 mg

* Percent Daily Values are based on a 2,000 calorie diet.

CROSSROADS BEEF

Ingredients

- 2 tsps garlic, diced
- 1/2 tsp prepared horseradish
- 1 tsp hot pepper sauce
- 1 tsp dried thyme
- 1/2 tsp salt
- 1/2 tsp ground black pepper
- 2 tsps Cajun seasoning
- 2 tbsps olive oil
- 2 tbsps malt vinegar
- 2 lbs beef eye of round roast

Directions

- Get a bowl, combine: malt vinegar, garlic, olive oil, horseradish, Cajun spice, hot sauce, pepper, salt, and thyme.
- Perforate the beef with a large fork then place the beef in a big plastic bag that can be sealed.
- Add in the oil mix and coat the meat evenly. Squeeze out any excess air in the bag then place the meat in the fridge for 8 hrs.
- Add the meat to the crock pot of a slow cooker and the marinade as well.
- Place the lid on the slow cooker and cook the meat for 9 hrs with low level of heat.
- Enjoy.

Amount per serving (8 total)

Timing Information:

Preparation	15 m
Cooking	8 h
Total Time	16 h 15 m

Nutritional Information:

Calories	148 kcal
Fat	9.7 g
Carbohydrates	1.1g
Protein	< 13.4 g
Cholesterol	36 mg
Sodium	311 mg

* Percent Daily Values are based on a 2,000 calorie diet.

Monday Night Meals

Authentic Texas Burgers

Ingredients

- 1/2 C. mayonnaise
- 1 tsp Cajun seasoning
- 1 1/3 lbs ground beef sirloin
- 1 jalapeno pepper, seeded and diced
- 1/2 C. diced white onion
- 1 clove garlic, minced
- 1 tbsp Cajun seasoning
- 1 tsp Worcestershire sauce
- 4 slices pepperjack cheese
- 4 hamburger buns, split
- 4 leaves lettuce
- 4 slices tomato

Directions

- Get your grill hot and oil the grate.
- Get a bowl, combine: 1 tbsp of Cajun spice and mayo.
- Get a 2nd bowl, combine: Worcestershire, beef, 1 tbsp Cajun spice, jalapenos, garlic, and onions.
- Now shape the beef mix into 4 burgers.
- Grill the burgers for 6 mins each side. Place a piece of cheese on each patty on the grill and heat them until the cheese melts.
- Coat your buns with the Cajun mayo, a beef patty, a piece of tomato, and some lettuce. Enjoy.

Amount per serving (4 total)

Timing Information:

Preparation	25 m
Cooking	15 m
Total Time	40 m

Nutritional Information:

Calories	714 kcal
Fat	49.1 g
Carbohydrates	28.5g
Protein	38.3 g
Cholesterol	132 mg
Sodium	1140 mg

* Percent Daily Values are based on a 2,000 calorie diet.

SPICY GARLIC TILAPIA

Ingredients

- 4 (4 oz.) fillets tilapia
- 4 cloves crushed garlic
- 3 tbsps olive oil
- 1 onion, diced
- 1/4 tsp cayenne pepper

Directions

- Take your pieces of garlic and rub the pieces of fish with it. Now place everything into a casserole dish.
- Coat your tilapia with olive oil and then layer your onions over everything.
- Place a covering around the dish and place everything in the fridge for 8 hrs.
- Set your oven to 350 degrees before doing anything else.
- Top your fish with the cayenne and cook everything in the oven for 32 mins.
- Enjoy.

Amount per serving (4 total)

Timing Information:

Preparation	5 m
Cooking	30 m
Total Time	1 d 35 m

Nutritional Information:

Calories	217 kcal
Fat	11.7 g
Carbohydrates	3.6g
Protein	23.5 g
Cholesterol	41 mg
Sodium	74 mg

* Percent Daily Values are based on a 2,000 calorie diet.

Lime and Mushrooms Tilapia

Ingredients

- 1 oz. dried porcini mushrooms
- 2 tbsps butter
- 2 (4 oz.) fillets tilapia, halved
- kosher salt to taste
- ground black pepper to taste
- 1 tbsp lemon zest
- 2 limes, juiced
- 2 green onions, diced

Directions

- For 25 mins let your mushrooms sit submerged, in water, in a bowl, then cut them up.
- Coat your fish with pepper, and kosher salt. Then fry it in half of your butter.
- Add in half of the zest, half of the lime juice, and cook everything for 7 mins.
- Turn over the piece of fish and coat it with more pepper, and more salt.
- Add the rest of the zest, the lime juice, the butter, mushrooms, and onions.
- Cook everything for 7 mins.
- Enjoy.

Amount per serving (4 total)

Timing Information:

Preparation	15 m
Cooking	10 m
Total Time	45 m

Nutritional Information:

Calories	146 kcal
Fat	6.9 g
Carbohydrates	8g
Protein	14.2 g
Cholesterol	36 mg
Sodium	322 mg

* Percent Daily Values are based on a 2,000 calorie diet.

CREAMY LEMON PEPPER TILAPIA

Ingredients

- 4 (4 oz.) fillets tilapia
- butter flavored cooking spray
- 4 tsps margarine, melted
- 2 tbsps lemon juice
- 2 tbsps diced fresh dill weed
- 1 tbsp lemon-pepper seasoning
- 4 tsps cream cheese
- 5 tbsps lemon juice, or to taste
- 2 tbsps diced fresh dill weed

Directions

- Set your oven to 375 degrees before doing anything else.
- Coat a casserole dish with nonstick spray and layer your pieces of fish in it.
- Now coat the fish with some spray as well as: lemon juice (2 tbsps), margarine, dill (2 tbsps), and lemon pepper.
- Cook everything in the oven for 17 mins.
- Now get a bowl, mix: remaining dill, cream cheese, and lemon juice (5 tbsps). Cook everything in the microwave for 90 secs. Then whisked the mix for 30 secs. When serving your fish top it with the sauce.
- Enjoy.

Amount per serving (4 total)

Timing Information:

Preparation	5 m
Cooking	25 m
Total Time	30 m

Nutritional Information:

Calories	173 kcal
Fat	7 g
Carbohydrates	3g
Protein	< 23.6 g
Cholesterol	47 mg
Sodium	480 mg

* Percent Daily Values are based on a 2,000 calorie diet.

Monterey Shrimp

Ingredients

- 1 (8 ounce) package Monterey Jack cheese, cut into strips
- 40 large shrimp - peeled, deveined and butterflied
- 20 slices bacon, cut in half

Directions

- Set your oven at 450 degrees F.
- Put cheese along with a slice of bacon in the butter flied opening of each shrimp before placing it on a cookie sheet.
- Bake this in the preheated oven for about 15 minutes.
- Serve.

Serving: 8

Timing Information:

Preparation	Cooking	Total Time
20 mins	10 mins	30 mins

Nutritional Information:

Calories	284 kcal
Carbohydrates	0.4 g
Cholesterol	205 mg
Fat	16.9 g
Fiber	0 g
Protein	30.7 g
Sodium	753 mg

* Percent Daily Values are based on a 2,000 calorie diet.

Szechwan Shrimp

Ingredients

- 4 tbsps water
- 2 tbsps ketchup
- 1 tbsp soy sauce
- 2 tsps cornstarch
- 1 tsp honey
- 1/2 tsp crushed red pepper
- 1/4 tsp ground ginger
- 1 tbsp vegetable oil
- 1/4 C. sliced green onions
- 4 cloves garlic, minced
- 12 ounces cooked shrimp, tails removed

Directions

- Combine water, crushed red pepper, ketchup, soy sauce, cornstarch, honey and ground ginger in a medium sized bowl and set it aside.
- Cook green onions and garlic in hot oil for about 30 seconds before adding shrimp and mixing it well.
- Now add sauce and cook until you see that the sauce has thickened.
- Serve.

Serving: 4

Timing Information:

Preparation	Cooking	Total Time
10 mins	10 mins	20 mins

Nutritional Information:

Calories	142 kcal
Carbohydrates	6.7 g
Cholesterol	164 mg
Fat	4.4 g
Fiber	0.4 g
Protein	18.3 g
Sodium	500 mg

* Percent Daily Values are based on a 2,000 calorie diet.

Shrimp Scampi

Ingredients

- 1 (8 ounce) package angel hair pasta
- 1/2 C. butter
- 4 cloves minced garlic
- 1 pound shrimp, peeled and deveined
- 1 C. dry white wine
- 1/4 tsp ground black pepper
- 3/4 C. grated Parmesan cheese
- 1 tbsp chopped fresh parsley

Directions

- Cook pasta in boiling salty water until tender before draining it.
- Now cook shrimp and garlic in hot butter over medium for about three minutes before adding wine and pepper, and cooking all this for another 30 seconds.
- Now combine pasta and shrimp in a bowl before adding cheese and parsley.
- Mix it thoroughly before serving.

Serving: 4

Timing Information:

Preparation	Cooking	Total Time
15 mins	10 mins	25 mins

Nutritional Information:

Calories	606 kcal
Carbohydrates	35.5 g
Cholesterol	247 mg
Fat	30.8 g
Fiber	2.1 g
Protein	35.3 g
Sodium	680 mg

* Percent Daily Values are based on a 2,000 calorie diet.

Maui Chicken

Ingredients

- 1 tbsp sesame or canola oil
- 1 lb chicken tenders, cut into 1-inch pieces
- 1 (2 inch) piece fresh ginger, peeled and cut into matchsticks or minced
- 4 cloves garlic, thinly sliced
- 1/2 C. dry sherry (see Tip)
- 1 (14 oz.) can reduced-sodium chicken broth
- 1 1/2 C. water
- 2 tbsps reduced-sodium soy sauce
- 1 tsp Asian red chili sauce, such as sriracha, or to taste
- 1 bunch mustard greens or chard, stemmed and diced

Directions

- Stir fry your chicken in a Dutch oven for 9 min.
- Then remove them from the pot. Combine in the garlic and the ginger and cook everything for 30 secs then add the sherry and fry the mix for 4 mins while scraping the pan. Now combine in the water and broth and get everything boiling with a high level of heat. Once the mix is boiling let it continue for 7 mins then add: chards, chili sauce, and soy sauce.
- Continue cooking this mix for 3 mins. Enjoy.

Amount per serving (4 total)

Timing Information:

Preparation	Cooking	Total Time
		35 m

Nutritional Information:

Calories	221 kcal
Fat	6.5 g
Carbohydrates	10.8g
Protein	26.6 g
Cholesterol	67 mg
Sodium	1048 mg

* Percent Daily Values are based on a 2,000 calorie diet.

Coconut Chicken

Ingredients

- 1 1/2 lbs skinless, boneless chicken breast halves - cut into 1 inch cubes
- 2 limes, zested and juiced
- 2 tbsps grated fresh ginger root
- 1 3/4 C. coconut milk
- 1/2 tsp white sugar
- 1 C. jasmine rice
- 1 tbsp sesame oil
- 1 tbsp honey
- 1/4 C. sweetened flaked coconut

Directions

- Get a bowl, combine: grated ginger, chicken breast, lime zest, and lime juice. Place a covering on the bowl and let the chicken marinate for 30 mins in the fridge.
- Get a saucepan and combine: sugar and milk. Get it lightly boiling then add in your jasmine rice. Set the high to low then place a lid on the pan and cook for 22 mins.
- Get a wok hot with sesame oil and then add in your chicken and the liquid. Cook for 5 mins stirring constantly with high heat.
- Add your honey and keep stirring so nothing burns.
- Shut off the heat and add in your coconut enjoy with rice.

Amount per serving (4 total)

Timing Information:

Preparation	Cooking	Total Time
15 m	25 m	1 h

Nutritional Information:

Calories	660 kcal
Fat	31.2 g
Carbohydrates	53g
Protein	43.8 g
Cholesterol	104 mg
Sodium	117 mg

* Percent Daily Values are based on a 2,000 calorie diet.

Asian Style Chicken with Plums

Ingredients

- 1 C. uncooked long grain white rice
- 2 C. water
- 2/3 C. plum sauce
- 1/2 C. light corn syrup
- 2 tbsps soy sauce
- 2 cloves garlic, minced
- 4 packets chicken bouillon granules
- 2 tbsps vegetable oil
- 4 skinless, boneless chicken breast halves - cut into bite-size pieces
- 4 tbsps cornstarch
- 3/4 tsp minced fresh ginger root
- 2 C. snow peas, trimmed
- 1 C. sliced fresh mushrooms

Directions

- Get your rice boiling in water, place a lid on the pot, set the heat to a low level, and let the contents cook for 22 mins.
- Get a bowl, mix: bouillon, plum sauce, garlic, corn syrup, and soy sauce.
- Coat your chicken with cornstarch and then fry it for 7 mins in hot oil or until it is fully done then add in: mushrooms, ginger, and snow peas.
- Cook the mix for 6 more mins or until the veggies are soft then add in the plum sauce. Enjoy.

Amount per serving (6 total)

Timing Information:

Preparation	Cooking	Total Time
15 m	25 m	40 m

Nutritional Information:

Calories	432 kcal
Fat	7.4 g
Carbohydrates	70.9g
Protein	20.5 g
Cholesterol	41 mg
Sodium	1283 mg

* Percent Daily Values are based on a 2,000 calorie diet.

Classical Alfredo

Ingredients

- 6 skinless, boneless chicken breast halves - cut into cubes
- 6 tbsps butter, divided
- 4 cloves garlic, minced, divided
- 1 tbsp Italian seasoning
- 1 lb fettuccini pasta
- 1 onion, diced
- 1 (8 oz.) package sliced mushrooms
- 1/3 C. all-purpose flour
- 1 tbsp salt
- 3/4 tsp ground white pepper
- 3 C. milk
- 1 C. half-and-half
- 3/4 C. grated Parmesan cheese
- 8 oz. shredded Colby-Monterey Jack cheese
- 3 roma (plum) tomatoes, diced
- 1/2 C. sour cream

Directions

- Stir your chicken after coating it with Italian seasoning in 2 tbsp of butter with 2 pieces of garlic.
- Stir fry the meat until it is fully done then place everything to the side.
- Now boil your pasta in water and salt for 9 mins then remove all the liquids.

- At the same time stir fry your onions in 4 tbsp of butter along with the mushrooms and 2 more pieces of garlic.
- Continue frying the mix until the onions are see-through then combine in your pepper, salt, and flour.
- Stir and cook the mix for 4 mins. Then gradually add in your half and half and the milk, while stirring, until everything is smooth.
- Combine in the Monterey and parmesan and let the mix cook until the cheese has melted then add the chicken, sour cream, and tomatoes.
- Serve your pasta topped liberally with the chicken mix and sauce.
- Enjoy.

Amount per serving (8 total)

Timing Information:

Preparation	30 m
Cooking	30 m
Total Time	1 h

Nutritional Information:

Calories	673 kcal
Fat	30.8 g
Carbohydrates	57g
Protein	43.3 g
Cholesterol	133 mg
Sodium	1386 mg

* Percent Daily Values are based on a 2,000 calorie diet.

Easy Italian Parmigiana

Ingredients

- 1 egg, beaten
- 2 oz. dry bread crumbs
- 2 skinless, boneless chicken breast halves
- 3/4 (16 oz.) jar spaghetti sauce
- 2 oz. shredded mozzarella cheese
- 1/4 C. grated Parmesan cheese

Directions

- Coat a cookie sheet with oil then set your oven to 350 degrees before doing anything else.
- Get a bowl and add in your eggs.
- Get a 2nd bowl and add in your bread crumbs.
- Coat your chicken first with the eggs then with the bread crumbs.
- Lay your pieces of chicken on the cookie sheet and cook them in the oven for 45 mins, until they are fully done.
- Now add half of your pasta sauce to a casserole dish and lay in your chicken on top of the sauce. Place the rest of the sauce on top of the chicken pieces. Then add a topping of parmesan and mozzarella over everything. Cook the parmigiana in the oven for 25 mins. Enjoy.

Amount per serving (2 total)

Timing Information:

Preparation	30 m
Cooking	1 h
Total Time	1 h 30 m

Nutritional Information:

Calories	528 kcal
Fat	18.3 g
Carbohydrates	44.9g
Protein	43.5 g
Cholesterol	184 mg
Sodium	1309 mg

* Percent Daily Values are based on a 2,000 calorie diet.

Maggie's Favorite Pasta

Ingredients

- 2 tbsps olive oil
- 1 anchovy fillet
- 2 tbsps capers
- 3 cloves minced garlic
- 1/2 C. dry white wine
- 1/4 tsp dried oregano
- 1 pinch red pepper flakes, or to taste
- 3 C. crushed Italian (plum) tomatoes
- salt and ground black pepper to taste
- 1 pinch cayenne pepper, or to taste
- 1 (7 oz.) can oil-packed tuna, drained
- 1/4 C. diced fresh flat-leaf parsley
- 1 (12 oz.) package spaghetti
- 1 tbsp extra-virgin olive oil, or to taste
- 1/4 C. freshly grated Parmigiano-Reggiano cheese, or to taste
- 1 tbsp diced fresh flat-leaf parsley, or to taste

Directions

- Stir fry your capers and anchovies in olive oil for 4 mins then combine in the garlic and continue frying the mix for 2 more mins.

- Now add: pepper flakes, white wine, and orange.
- Stir the mix and turn up the heat.
- Let the mix cook for 5 mins before adding the tomatoes and getting the mix to a gentle simmer.
- Once the mix is simmering add in: cayenne, black pepper, and salt.
- Set the heat to low and let everything cook for 12 mins.
- Now begin to boil your pasta in water and salt for 10 mins then remove all the liquids and leave the noodles in the pan.
- Combine the simmering tomatoes with the noodles and place a lid on the pot. With a low level of heat warm everything for 4 mins.
- When serving your pasta top it with some Parmigiano-Reggiano, parsley, and olive oil.
- Enjoy.

Amount per serving (4 total)

Timing Information:

Preparation	20 m
Cooking	35 m
Total Time	55 m

Nutritional Information:

Calories	619 kcal
Fat	17.7 g
Carbohydrates	79.5g
Protein	31.2 g
Cholesterol	14 mg
Sodium	706 mg

* Percent Daily Values are based on a 2,000 calorie diet.

Classical Lasagna I

Ingredients

- 1 1/2 lbs lean ground beef
- 1 onion, diced
- 2 cloves garlic, minced
- 1 tbsp diced fresh basil
- 1 tsp dried oregano
- 2 tbsps brown sugar
- 1 1/2 tsps salt
- 1 (29 oz.) can diced tomatoes
- 2 (6 oz.) cans tomato paste
- 12 dry lasagna noodles
- 2 eggs, beaten
- 1 pint part-skim ricotta cheese
- 1/2 C. grated Parmesan cheese
- 2 tbsps dried parsley
- 1 tsp salt
- 1 lb mozzarella cheese, shredded
- 2 tbsps grated Parmesan cheese

Directions

- Stir fry your garlic, onions, and beef for 3 mins then combine in: tomato paste, basil, diced tomatoes, oregano, 1.5 tsp salt, and brown sugar.
- Now set your oven to 375 degrees before doing anything else.
- Begin to boil your pasta in water and salt for 9 mins then remove all the liquids.

- Get a bowl, combine: 1 tsp salt, eggs, parsley, ricotta, and parmesan.
- Place a third of the pasta in a casserole dish and top everything with half of the cheese mix, one third of the sauce, and 1/2 of the mozzarella.
- Continue layering in this manner until all the ingredients have been used up.
- Then top everything with some more parmesan.
- Cook the lasagna in the oven for 35 mins.
- Enjoy.

Amount per serving (8 total)

Timing Information:

Preparation	30 m
Cooking	1 h 30 m
Total Time	2 h

Nutritional Information:

Calories	664 kcal
Fat	29.5 g
Carbohydrates	48.3g
Protein	50.9 g
Cholesterol	1168 mg
Sodium	1900 mg

* Percent Daily Values are based on a 2,000 calorie diet.

Chicken Marsala Classico

Ingredients

- 1/4 C. all-purpose flour for coating
- 1/2 tsp salt
- 1/4 tsp ground black pepper
- 1/2 tsp dried oregano
- 4 skinless, boneless chicken breast halves – flattened to 1/4 inch thick
- 4 tbsps butter
- 4 tbsps olive oil
- 1 C. sliced mushrooms
- 1/2 C. Marsala wine
- 1/4 C. cooking sherry

Directions

- Get a bowl, combine: oregano, flour, pepper, and salt.
- Dredge your pieces of chicken in the mix then begin to stir fry the chicken in butter.
- Let the chicken fry until it is browned all over then add in: the sherry, mushrooms, and wine.
- Place a lid on the pan and let the contents gently boil for 12 mins.
- Enjoy.

Amount per serving (4 total)

Timing Information:

Preparation	10 m
Cooking	20 m
Total Time	30 m

Nutritional Information:

Calories	448 kcal
Fat	26.6 g
Carbohydrates	13.3g
Protein	28.8 g
Cholesterol	99 mg
Sodium	543 mg

* Percent Daily Values are based on a 2,000 calorie diet.

CHIPOTLE CHILI

Ingredients

- 2 lbs lean ground beef
- 1 onion, diced
- 2 red bell peppers, seeded and diced
- 2 jalapeno peppers, seeded and diced
- 4 cloves garlic, minced
- 1/2 C. chili powder
- 1/4 C. ground cumin
- 1 tsp salt
- 1 tsp ground black pepper
- 1 (6 oz.) can tomato paste
- 4 (15 oz.) cans kidney beans with liquid
- 1 (14.5 oz.) can Italian-style stewed tomatoes
- 1 (7 oz.) can chipotle peppers in adobo sauce
- 1 quart water, divided
- 1/4 C. all-purpose flour
- 1 tbsp rice vinegar

Directions

- Blend your adobo chilies until paste like for about 3 to 5 mins. Then place them to the side.
- Get a bowl, mix until smooth: 1 C. of water, and flour.

- Stir fry your beef until fully done then add in: chili powder, beans, jalapenos, tomato paste, cumin, onions, salt, garlic, pepper, and bell pepper.
- Stir and cook this mix for about 3 mins, and then add in the puree and also water (3 C.).
- Cook everything for 2 mins before adding the flour and the water mix. Stir everything before adding the vinegar.
- Get the mix boiling and then reduce the heat to a gentle simmering. Let the chili cook for 50 mins.
- Enjoy.

Amount per serving (16 total)

Timing Information:

Preparation	20 m
Cooking	1 h
Total Time	1 h 20 m

Nutritional Information:

Calories	295 kcal
Fat	13.5 g
Carbohydrates	27.1g
Protein	17.6 g
Cholesterol	43 mg
Sodium	649 mg

* Percent Daily Values are based on a 2,000 calorie diet.

Easy Rustic Chili

Ingredients

- 4 skinless, boneless chicken breast halves
- 1 (16 oz.) jar salsa
- 2 tsps garlic powder
- 1 tsp ground cumin
- 1 tsp chili powder
- salt to taste
- ground black pepper to taste
- 1 (11 oz.) can Mexican-style corn
- 1 (15 oz.) can pinto beans

Directions

- Get a bowl, mix: chicken, pepper, garlic powder, salt, chili powder, and cumin.
- Now cook your salsa and chicken for 7 hours with a low heat in the slow cooker.
- After the meat has cooked for 4 hours take it out of the slow cooker and shred it.
- Place it back in the crock pot along with the beans and corn and continue cooking.
- Enjoy.

Amount per serving (6 total)

Timing Information:

Preparation	15 m
Cooking	12 h
Total Time	12 h 15 m

Nutritional Information:

Calories	188 kcal
Fat	2.3 g
Carbohydrates	22.6g
Protein	20.4 g
Cholesterol	41 mg
Sodium	1012 mg

* Percent Daily Values are based on a 2,000 calorie diet.

Turkey, Salsa, and Zucchini Chili

Ingredients

- 3 tbsps vegetable oil, divided
- 1 1/2 lbs ground turkey
- 1 (1 oz.) package taco seasoning mix
- 1 tsp ground coriander
- 1 tsp dried oregano
- 1 tsp chili pepper flakes
- 2 tbsps tomato paste
- 1 (14.5 oz.) can beef broth
- 1 (7 oz.) can salsa
- 1 (14.5 oz.) can crushed tomatoes, or coarsely diced tomatoes packed in puree
- 1 (7 oz.) can diced green chili peppers
- 1 medium onion, finely diced
- 1 green bell pepper, diced
- 3 medium zucchini, halved lengthwise and sliced
- 1 bunch green onions, diced
- 1 C. sour cream
- 1 C. shredded Cheddar cheese

Directions

- Stir fry your turkey in oil after adding the following to it first: tomato paste, taco seasoning, chili flakes, coriander, and oregano.
- Cook the turkey until you have browned it and then add in the broth and boil the contents for 7 mins.

- Now add: green chilies, tomatoes, and salsa.
- Meanwhile in a separate pan stir fry: bell peppers, and onions for 6 mins then combine it with the chili.
- Reduce the heat on the chili to low level and gently boil everything.
- Now, stir fry for 6 mins, your zucchini in oil, then pour it in with the chili.
- Cook the chili for about 17 more mins and add some water if you find that it is too thick for your liking.
- When serving your chili add the following to each serving: cheddar, green onions, and a dollop of sour cream.
- Enjoy.

Amount per serving (6 total)

Timing Information:

Preparation	15 m
Cooking	55 m
Total Time	1 h 10 m

Nutritional Information:

Calories	506 kcal
Fat	31.9 g
Carbohydrates	24.1g
Protein	34.7 g
Cholesterol	125 mg
Sodium	1521 mg

* Percent Daily Values are based on a 2,000 calorie diet.

Italian Cabbage I

Ingredients

- 1 tbsp olive oil
- 1 large onion, diced
- 1 1/2 lbs ground beef
- 1 tsp garlic powder
- 1/2 tsp red pepper flakes
- 1/2 tsp Italian seasoning
- salt and pepper to taste
- 1 small head cabbage, diced
- 2 (14.5 ounce) cans diced tomatoes
- 1 (14.5 ounce) can tomato sauce

Directions

- Cook onion in hot oil for about 5 minutes before adding ground beef and cooking it for another seven minutes or until brown.
- Simmer garlic powder, red pepper flakes, Italian seasoning, salt, cabbage, diced tomatoes, and tomato for a few mins in the pot. Before cooking it for another 25 minutes and adding salt and pepper.
- Serve.

Serving: 10

Timing Information:

Preparation	Cooking	Total Time
10 mins	35 mins	45 mins

Nutritional Information:

Calories	178 kcal
Carbohydrates	8.7 g
Cholesterol	43 mg
Fat	9.7 g
Fiber	2.8 g
Protein	13.3 g
Sodium	204 mg

* Percent Daily Values are based on a 2,000 calorie diet.

Classical Enchiladas

Ingredients

- 1 1/2 lbs lean ground beef
- 1 bunch green onions, finely chopped
- 1 diced fresh jalapeno pepper, or to taste
- 1/4 cup water
- 1 package taco seasoning mix
- 1 cup plain yogurt
- 1 can condensed cream of chicken soup
- 2 cups shredded mozzarella
- 6 corn tortillas

Directions

- Set your oven at 350 degrees F before doing anything else.
- Cook ground beef, jalapeno and green onion over medium heat until you see that it is brown before adding taco seasoning and water, and continue cooking until the water evaporates.
- Put this mixture along with two tbsps of a mixture of yoghurt, cheese and condensed soup over the meat very neatly between tortillas before placing it in the baking dish.
- Do the same thing with all the other tortillas.
- Bake this in the preheated oven for about 30 minutes.
- Serve.

Serving: 6

Timing Information:

Preparation	Cooking	Total Time
15 mins	40 mins	55 mins

Nutritional Information:

Calories	556 kcal
Carbohydrates	26.1 g
Cholesterol	116 mg
Fat	33.8 g
Fiber	2.7 g
Protein	34.8 g
Sodium	1122 mg

* Percent Daily Values are based on a 2,000 calorie diet.

Cantonese Ground Beef

Ingredients

- 1 lb ground beef
- 1 can condensed cream of mushroom soup
- 1 can condensed cream of celery soup
- 1 can sliced water chestnuts, drained
- 1 cup diced celery
- 3/4 cup water
- 2/3 cup shredded Colby-Monterey Jack cheese
- 1/2 cup sliced almonds
- 1/2 cup sliced mushrooms
- 2 tbsps soy sauce
- 1/2 tsp ground black pepper
- 1 can chow mein noodles

Directions

- Set your oven at 350 degrees F and put some oil on the baking dish.
- Cook beef over medium heat for about 7 minutes or until brown.
- Combine beef, mushroom soup, mushrooms, celery soup, soy sauce, water chestnuts, celery, water, Monterey Jack cheese, almonds and black pepper together in the baking dish before covering it up with aluminum foil.

- Bake this in the preheated oven for about 45 minutes before adding chow mein noodles on top of the casserole and baking it for 30 more minutes.
- Serve.

Serving: 6

Timing Information:

Preparation	Cooking	Total Time
10 mins	1 hr 20 mins	1 hr 30 mins

Nutritional Information:

Calories	488 kcal
Carbohydrates	29 g
Cholesterol	67 mg
Fat	31.1 g
Fiber	4 g
Protein	23.7 g
Sodium	1368 mg

* Percent Daily Values are based on a 2,000 calorie diet.

Lemongrass Beef

Ingredients

- 1/2 cup coarsely chopped lemon grass
- 1 onion, coarsely chopped
- 2 cloves garlic
- 1 1/2 lbs lean ground beef
- 1 tsp salt
- 1/2 tsp ground black pepper
- 1 tsp white sugar
- 1 tbsp cornstarch
- 1 tbsp oyster sauce
- 1 tsp sesame oil

Directions

- At first you need to set a grill to medium heat and put some oil before starting anything else.
- Blend a mixture of lemon grass, garlic and onion in a blender for about ten seconds before adding beef, salt, pepper, sugar, cornstarch, oyster sauce, and sesame oil into the bowl containing blended mixture.
- Make approx. twelve meatballs out of it before threading them into skewers.
- Cook this on the preheated grill for about seven minutes each side.
- Serve.

Serving: 12

Timing Information:

Preparation	Cooking	Total Time
15 mins	15 mins	30 mins

Nutritional Information:

Calories	392 kcal
Carbohydrates	8.3 g
Cholesterol	111 mg
Fat	24.8 g
Fiber	0.6 g
Protein	32.1 g
Sodium	709 mg

* Percent Daily Values are based on a 2,000 calorie diet.

Italian Cabbage II

Ingredients

- 1 large head cabbage, finely chopped
- 1 (14.5 ounce) can diced tomatoes with juice
- 1 onion, halved and thinly sliced
- 1 tbsp Italian seasoning
- salt and ground black pepper to taste
- 1 lb lean ground beef

Directions

- Cook a mixture of cabbage, Italian seasoning, tomatoes with juice, onion, salt and black pepper over low heat for a few minutes before adding ground beef and cooking all this for 45 minutes or until the cabbage is tender.
- Serve.

Timing Information:

Preparation	Cooking	Total Time
10 mins	35 mins	45 mins

Nutritional Information:

Calories	228 kcal
Carbohydrates	18.3 g
Cholesterol	50 mg
Fat	9.5 g
Fiber	6.7 g
Protein	18.1 g
Sodium	255 mg

* Percent Daily Values are based on a 2,000 calorie diet.

Sweet and Sour Ground Beef

Ingredients

- 1 lb ground beef
- 1/4 cup yellow mustard
- 1 tbsp balsamic vinegar
- 1 tbsp minced garlic
- 1 1/2 tsps soy sauce
- 1 1/2 tsps honey
- 1 1/2 tsps paprika
- 1/8 tsp ground black pepper

Directions

- Cook beef over medium heat in a skillet for about seven minutes or until brown before adding mustard, paprika, balsamic vinegar, garlic, soy sauce, honey, and black pepper, and cooking all this for another three minutes.
- Serve.

Serving: 6

Timing Information:

Preparation	Cooking	Total Time
10 mins	5 mins	15 mins

Nutritional Information:

Calories	233 kcal
Carbohydrates	5.1 g
Cholesterol	71 mg
Fat	14.4 g
Fiber	0.9 g
Protein	20.2 g
Sodium	356 mg

* Percent Daily Values are based on a 2,000 calorie diet.

Ground Beef Macaroni

Ingredients

- 1 1/2 lbs lean ground beef
- 1 green bell pepper, diced
- 1 onion, diced
- 2 (29 ounce) cans tomato sauce
- 1 (16 ounce) package macaroni

Directions

- Cook pasta according to the directions of package before draining it using a colander.
- Cook ground beef over medium heat until brown before adding chopped onion and cooking it for another few minutes to get them soft.
- Now add tomato sauce and green pepper before cooking it until pepper is soft.
- Pour this sauce over pasta for serving.

Serving: 6

Timing Information:

Preparation	Cooking	Total Time
30 mins	30 mins	1 hr

Nutritional Information:

Calories	570 kcal
Carbohydrates	72.9 g
Cholesterol	74 mg
Fat	15.5 g
Fiber	6.8 g
Protein	35.2 g
Sodium	1492 mg

* Percent Daily Values are based on a 2,000 calorie diet.

Buffalo Wings I

Ingredients

- oil for deep frying
- 1 C. unbleached all-purpose flour
- 2 tsps salt
- 1/2 tsp ground black pepper
- 1/2 tsp cayenne pepper
- 1/4 tsp garlic powder
- 1/2 tsp paprika
- 1 egg
- 1 C. milk
- 3 skinless, boneless chicken breasts, cut into 1/2-inch strips
- 1/4 C. hot pepper sauce
- 1 tbsp butter

Directions

- Get your oil hot for frying.
- At the same time get a bowl, combine: paprika, flour, garlic powder, salt, cayenne, and black pepper.
- Get a 2nd bowl, combine: milk and eggs.
- Coat your chicken first with the gg mix then dredge them in the flour mix.
- Place the chicken back in the egg mix and again in the flour mix.
- Place everything in a bowl and place a covering of plastic on the bowl.

- Put the chicken in the fridge for 30 mins then begin to fry the chicken, in batches, for 8 mins.
- Once all the chicken is done get a 3rd bowl and combine your butter and hot sauce.
- Place the mix in the microwave for 1 min with a high level of heat then top the chicken with the mix.
- Enjoy.

Amount per serving (3 total)

Timing Information:

Preparation	10 m
Cooking	20 m
Total Time	50 m

Nutritional Information:

Calories	710 kcal
Fat	46.9 g
Carbohydrates	43.7g
Protein	28 g
Cholesterol	136 mg
Sodium	2334 mg

* Percent Daily Values are based on a 2,000 calorie diet.

Buffalo Chicken Sandwich

Ingredients

- 1 tbsp vegetable oil
- 1 tbsp butter
- 1 lb skinless, boneless chicken breasts, cut into bite-size pieces
- 1/4 C. hot sauce
- 4 (10 inch) flour tortillas
- 2 C. shredded lettuce
- 1 celery stalk, diced
- 1/2 C. blue cheese dressing

Directions

- Fry your chicken in veggie oil for 12 mins until it is fully done then place the meat to the side in a bowl.
- Add in the hot sauce to the bowl and stir everything to evenly coat the meat.
- Now place your tortillas on a working surface and place your chicken on each equally.
- Layer your dressing, celery, and lettuce over everything then form the contents into burritos.
- Enjoy.

Amount per serving (4 total)

Timing Information:

Preparation	20 m
Cooking	10 m
Total Time	30 m

Nutritional Information:

Calories	588 kcal
Fat	32.6 g
Carbohydrates	39.8g
Protein	30.4 g
Cholesterol	83 mg
Sodium	1208 mg

* Percent Daily Values are based on a 2,000 calorie diet.

Buffalo Pizza

Ingredients

- 3 skinless, boneless chicken breast halves, cooked and cubed
- 2 tbsps butter, melted
- 1 (2 oz.) bottle hot sauce
- 1 (8 oz.) bottle blue cheese salad dressing
- 1 (16 inch) prepared pizza crust
- 1 (8 oz.) package shredded mozzarella cheese

Directions

- Set your oven to 425 degrees before doing anything else.
- Get a bowl, combine: hot sauce, butter, and chicken. Stir the mix until the chicken is evenly coated.
- Now lay out your pizza crust on a cookie sheet and coat it evenly with the ranch dressing.
- Add the chicken over the dressing, then add the cheese.
- Cook everything into the oven for 12 mins.
- Enjoy.

Amount per serving (6 total)

Timing Information:

Preparation	30 m
Cooking	25 m
Total Time	55 m

Nutritional Information:

Calories	785 kcal
Fat	40.7 g
Carbohydrates	66.6g
Protein	37.1 g
Cholesterol	83 mg
Sodium	1840 mg

* Percent Daily Values are based on a 2,000 calorie diet.

Florida Style Pierogi

Ingredients

- 4 1/2 tsps hot pepper sauce
- 1 tbsp vegetable oil
- 1/2 tsp chili powder
- 1 package frozen pierogi
- bleu cheese dressing
- celery rib

Directions

- Coat a casserole dish with nonstick spray then set your oven to 400 degrees before doing anything else.
- Get a bowl, combine: chili powder, hot sauce, and oil.
- Stir the mix until it is smooth then add in the pierogis and stir everything again.
- Place the contents in the dish and cook the pierogis for 22 mins in the oven.
- After 12 mins of cooking flip them.
- Divide your pierogis between serving dishes and also add some celery and blue cheese.
- Enjoy.

Amount per serving: 3

Timing Information:

Preparation	5 mins
Total Time	25 mins

Nutritional Information:

Calories	42.2
Cholesterol	0.0mg
Sodium	190.7mg
Carbohydrates	0.3g
Protein	0.0g

* Percent Daily Values are based on a 2,000 calorie diet.

Emily's Marsala

Ingredients

- 6 chicken breasts
- Salt
- Pepper
- Thyme
- 6 slices prosciutto
- 6 slices Fontina cheese
- Flour
- Canola oil
- 10 oz. sliced mushrooms
- 1 C. Marsala wine
- 4 C. chicken stock
- 1 tbsp butter
- 1 tbsp flour

Directions

- Slice an opening into your pieces of chicken then add in the thyme, pepper, and salt to them. Then add a piece of fontina, and prosciutto to each.
- Dredge the chicken in some flour then brown the chicken all over in oil.
- Place the chicken to the side.
- Begin to stir fry your mushrooms for 4 mins until they are browned then add in the marsala and cook everything for 7 mins.
- Add the stock then add the chicken to the mix as well.

- Let everything gently boil for 7 mins then place the meat on a serving dish.
- Add your butter and some flour to the sauce.
- Stir and heat the mix until it is thick.
- Top your chicken liberally with the sauce.
- Enjoy.

Amount per serving: 6

Timing Information:

Preparation	10 mins
Total Time	35 mins

Nutritional Information:

Calories	613.7
Cholesterol	135.1mg
Sodium	570.0mg
Carbohydrates	13.9g
Protein	43.1g

* Percent Daily Values are based on a 2,000 calorie diet.

Panhandle Seafood Sampler

Ingredients

- 2 1/2 C. water
- 3/4 lb unpeeled medium raw shrimp
- 1 (8 oz.) packages cream cheese, softened
- 1/4 C. lemon juice
- 1 tbsp mayonnaise
- 1/2 tsp seasoning salt
- 1/2 tsp lemon-pepper seasoning
- 1/4 tsp Worcestershire sauce
- 1 (12 oz.) jars seafood cocktail sauce
- 2 C. shredded monterey jack cheese
- 3 green onions, chopped
- 1/2 C. chopped green bell pepper
- 1/2 C. sliced ripe black olives

Directions

- Get your shrimp boiling in water for 7 mins then remove the liquids.
- Remove the skins of your shrimp and also take out the veins.
- Slice the shrimp into two pieces and dice half of the pieces.
- Place all the shrimp in a bowl and place a covering of plastic over everything.
- Put the shrimp in the fridge until everything is cold.

- Add your cream cheese to the bowl of a food processor and with an electric mixer, stir the cheese until it is light and frothy then combine in the Worcestershire, lemon juice, lemon pepper, mayo, and seasoned salt.
- Mix everything until it is smooth then spread the mix over a serving dish.
- Place a covering of plastic over the dish and put everything in the fridge for 35 mins.
- Top the cheese mix with the cocktail sauce then place some of the shrimp over everything.
- Now layer the olives, bell pepper, and green onions, then add the rest of the shrimp.
- Place a covering on the dish again and place everything in the fridge until it is cold again.
- Serve with crackers or toasted bread.
- Enjoy.

Amount per serving: 25

Timing Information:

Preparation	15 mins
Total Time	15 mins

Nutritional Information:

Calories	87.0
Cholesterol	38.8mg
Sodium	124.5mg
Carbohydrates	1.2g
Protein	5.7g

* Percent Daily Values are based on a 2,000 calorie diet.

Authentic Cuban Sandwich II

Ingredients

Mayo:

- 1 1/2 C. mayonnaise
- 1/2 C. sour cream
- 1/4 C. chopped fresh cilantro
- 1/4 C. diced green onions
- 1 1/2 tbsps ground chipotle peppers
- 1 tbsp lime juice
- 1 tbsp butter and garlic powder (1/2 tsp) mixed
- 1 tsp ground cumin
- salt and ground black pepper to taste

Fillings:

- 2 tbsps olive oil
- 2 sweet onions, sliced
- 1 tsp red pepper flakes
- 1 tsp dried oregano
- 2 jalapeno peppers cut into rings, divided
- 4 ciabatta sandwich rolls, sliced horizontally
- 1/4 C. sweet hot mustard, divided
- 1/2 lb sliced Swiss cheese, divided
- 1/2 lb sliced deli roast pork loin, divided
- 1/2 lb sliced ham, divided
- 2 dill pickles, cut into strips lengthwise, divided

Directions

- Get a bowl, mix: black pepper, mayo, salt, sour cream, cumin, cilantro, garlic spread, green onions, lime juice, and chipotle peppers.
- Place a covering of plastic on the bowl and put everything in the fridge for 60 mins.
- Now set your oven to 500 degrees before doing anything else.
- Begin to stir fry your oregano, pepper flakes, and onions, in olive oil, for 7 mins, then add some black pepper and salt.
- Combine in half of the jalapenos and cook them for 5 mins. Then combine in the rest.
- Coat your pieces of bread with 1 tbsp of mustard and 2 tbsps of mayo mix.
- Layer some Swiss cheese, jalapenos, pork loin, pickles, and ham evenly amongst the sandwiches.
- Then top everything with the onion mix.
- Layer everything into a casserole dish and the contents in the oven for 6 mins.
- Enjoy.

Amount per serving (8 total)

Timing Information:

Preparation	30 m
Cooking	15 m
Total Time	1 h 45 m

Nutritional Information:

Calories	671 kcal
Fat	52.7 g
Carbohydrates	26.9g
Protein	24.2 g
Cholesterol	85 mg
Sodium	927 mg

* Percent Daily Values are based on a 2,000 calorie diet.

Classical Spanish Beef Patties

Ingredients

- 3 tbsps olive oil
- 1 lb ground beef
- 1 1/2 C. diced fresh cilantro
- 1 onion, diced
- 4 cloves garlic, minced
- 1 green bell pepper, diced
- 1 (8 oz.) can tomato sauce
- 1 (16 oz.) package egg roll wrappers
- 2 quarts vegetable oil for frying

Directions

- Stir fry your bell pepper, onions, and garlic in olive oil until tender.
- Combine in the meat and cook the meat until it is fully done.
- Now add the cilantro and tomato sauce.
- Heat the contents until the cilantro is soft then place everything to the side.
- Now add 3 tbsps of the meat mix into an egg roll wrapper and shape the wrapper into a triangle.
- Continue doing this until all your meat has been used up.
- Now deep fry these patties in hot veggie oil until golden on both sides. Then place the patties on some paper towels before serving.
- Enjoy.

Amount per serving (8 total)

Timing Information:

Preparation	15 m
Cooking	30 m
Total Time	45 m

Nutritional Information:

Calories	522 kcal
Fat	34.7 g
Carbohydrates	36.7g
Protein	15.9 g
Cholesterol	40 mg
Sodium	505 mg

* Percent Daily Values are based on a 2,000 calorie diet.

Thanks for Reading! Join the Club and Keep on Cooking with 6 More Cookbooks....

http://bit.ly/1TdrStv

To grab the box sets simply follow the link mentioned above, or tap one of book covers.

This will take you to a page where you can simply enter your email address and a PDF version of the box sets will be emailed to you.

Hope you are ready for some serious cooking!

http://bit.ly/1TdrStv

Come On...
Let's Be Friends :)

We adore our readers and love connecting with them socially.

Like BookSumo on Facebook and let's get social!

Facebook

And also check out the BookSumo Cooking Blog.

Food Lover Blog

Printed in Great Britain
by Amazon